MW00528163

100 Best Flies for Montana Trout

100 BEST FLIES FOR MONTANA TROUT

Compiled and edited by Thomas R. Pero
Photographs by Ted Fauceglia

First Edition

Library of Congress Cataloging-in-Publication Data

Pero, Thomas R.

100 Best Flies for Montana Trout./Thomas R. Pero (editor).—1st ed.

p. cm.

ISBN 9780974642772

Trout. 2. Fly fishing. I. Title.

Library of Congress Control Number: 2008930937

Book and cover design by John Cole Graphic Designer
Photographs of flies by Ted Fauceglia
Cover photograph by Brian O'Keefe

Published by Wild River Press, Post Office Box 13360, Mill Creek, Washington 98082 USA

Wild River Press Web site address: www.wildriverpress.com

Printed in China through Four Colour Imports, Ltd.

10 9 8 7 6 5 4 3 2 1

WILD RIVER PRESS is pleased to present this practical collection of 100 top fly patterns effective for trout in and on the wonderful waters of Montana. They are listed by broad category according to type (dry fly, nymph, etc.) and in alphabetical order within each category. This is not intended as an all-inclusive or exclusive list but, rather, a solid foundation from which you can pick and choose your favorites. Wherever and whenever you fish, you'll find many useful additions to your fly box. These flies all work; at times and under the right conditions, they are deadly. For recommendations of both proven traditional and innovative new patterns, thank you to experienced fly designers and avid anglers John Bailey of Dan Bailey, Craig Mathews of Blue Ribbon Flies, Dean Reiner of Hatch Finders Fly Shop, Duncan Oswald of Montana Fly Company, Marty Downey of Riverborn Fly Company, and Michael Hoiness of Yellowstone Fly Goods—no angler should go fishless with this premium selection. Good fishing!

DRY FLIES

Adams Quad

Tied by Dan Bailey

HOOK:	Dai-Riki #305, size 14-18
THREAD:	Gray 8/0
TAIL:	Dark dun Hi-Vis Floater
WING:	Medium dun turkey flats
BODY:	Natural gray goose biot
HACKLE:	Mixed grizzly and brown
THORAX:	Adams dubbing

Adams Parachute

Tied by Dan Bailey

HOOK:	Dai-Riki #305, size 12-20
THREAD:	Gray 8/0
TAIL:	Grizzly and brown hackle fibers
WING:	White calf body hair
BODY:	Adams gray dubbing
HACKLE:	Mixed grizzly and brown

Blue-Wing Olive Biot Parachute

Tied by Dan Bailey

HOOK:	Dai-Riki #320, size 16-20
THREAD:	Olive 8/0
TAIL:	Olive Microfibetts
WING:	White Antron yarn
BODY:	Olive turkey biot
THORAX:	Blue-wing olive dubbing
HACKLE:	Dun

Bullet Foam Stonefly

Tied by Riverborn Fly Company

HOOK:	Daiichi #1270, size 4-8
THREAD:	Orange 3/0
TAIL:	Round-segment orange foam colored with brown marking on side of segments
RIBBING:	Orange 3/0 thread
HACKLE:	Natural deer hair collar
WING:	Orange Krystal Flash underwing with white foam and black deer hair on top; tint white foam with orange marking pen and then add black dots with black Sharpie pen.
LEGS:	Black round rubber
HEAD:	Natural deer hair tied in bullet shape

Carlson's Purple Haze Chute

Tied by Montana Fly Company

HOOK:	Bronze standard dry-fly MFC #7000, size 14
THREAD:	Purple Uni
POST:	White calf tail
TAIL:	Natural elk mane
BODY:	Purple MFC Wonderwrap
THORAX:	Purple MFC Wonderwrap
HACKLE:	Brown and grizzly

Christiaens GT Adult Green Drake

Tied by Montana Fly Company

HOOK:	Bronze up-eye scud MFC #7009, size 10
THREAD:	Olive dun Uni 6/0
POST:	Smoke MFC Widow's Web
TAIL:	Brown tail fibers
UNDERBODY:	Light olive MFC Wabbit dubbing
ABDOMEN:	Blue-wing olive turkey biot
THORAX:	Light olive MFC Wabbit dubbing
HACKLE:	Grizzly dyed olive

Christiaens GT Adult Pale Morning Dun

Tied by Montana Fly Company

HOOK:	Bronze up-eye scud MFC #7009, size 14
THREAD:	Light Cahill Uni 6/0
POST:	Silver MFC Widow's Web
TAIL:	White Microfibbetts
ABDOMEN:	Pale morning dun turkey biot
HACKLE:	Cream
THORAX:	Light Cahill MFC Frog's Hair

Delektable CDC Holographic Olive Elk Hair Caddis

Tied by Riverborn Fly Company

HOOK:	Daiichi #1170 standard dry-fly, size 16
THREAD:	Olive waxed Danville 6/0
RIBBING:	Fine gold wire
BODY:	Holographic olive Ice Dubbing
LEGS:	Nymph-size solid brown Sili Legs
UNDERWING:	Dun or gray CDC
OVERWING:	Light bull elk
COLLAR:	Holographic olive Ice Dubbing. After tying the wing, dub over wraps and then apply a small amount of super glue to thread. Wrap thread several times so it sinks into the dubbing. Cut thread to finish. Super glue will secure thread.

Delekable Olive/Gold Twisted Sister

Tied by Riverborn Fly Company

HOOK:	Daiichi #1280 2XL 1X fine, size 8-18
THREAD:	Brown waxed Danville 6/0
TAIL:	Light natural bull elk
RIBBING:	Small amber Ultra Wire
ABDOMEN:	Olive Beartooth foam strips
BODY HACKLE:	Mixed brown and grizzly
THORAX:	Gold Beartooth foam strips; using a brown Sharpie fine-point marker, dot the body with small dots.
LEGS:	Pumkin-colored Sili Legs, nymph-size with brown barring and green-speckled flakes
UNDERWING:	Mottled-web synthetic fly film tied tent-style
OVERWING:	Light bull elk hair tied slightly longer than synthetic wing
EYES:	White calf tail pulled over bullet-style, same length as elk
COLLAR:	Peacock Ice Dubbing. After tying the wing, dub over wraps and then apply a small amount of super glue to thread. Wrap thread several times so it sinks into the dubbing. Cut thread to finish. Super glue will secure thread.

Delektable Orange/Brown Twisted "X"

Tied by Riverborn Fly Company

HOOK:	Daiichi #1280 2XL 1X fine, size 8-18
THREAD:	Brown waxed Danville 6/0
RIBBING:	Small amber Ultra Wire
ABDOMEN:	Orange Beartooth foam strips—size 8-18 for the bodies of flies size 8-12, larger for size 6 hook
PARACHUTE WING:	White Neer Hair
THORAX:	Brown Beartooth foam strips—size 8-18 for the bodies of flies size 8-12, larger foam for size 6 hook
LEGS:	Pumpkin-colored Sili Legs, nymph-size with brown barring and green-speckled flakes
HACKLES:	Mixed brown and grizzly
UNDERWING:	Mottled-web synthetic fly firm tied tent-style
OVERWING:	Light bull elk hair tied slightly longer than synthetic wing
COLLAR:	Peacock Ice Dubbing. After tying the wing, dub over wraps and then apply a small amount of super glue to thread. Wrap thread several times so it sinks into the dubbing. Cut thread to finish. Super glue will secure thread.

Delektable Red Worm

Tied by Riverborn Fly Company

HOOK:	Daiichi #1120 wide-gape scud hook, size 8-16
BEAD HEAD:	Gold bead to match size of hook
THREAD:	Red waxed Danville 6/0
FRONT SECTION:	Regular-size red Vernille or Ultra Chenille; tie this section first before adding bead.
MAINBODY:	Regular-size red Vernille or Ultra Chenille
OVERBODY:	Regular-size red Ice Stretch Lace
HACKLE:	Black-and-white-barred Hungarian partridge
COLLAR:	Red Ice Dub to match dubbing. Dub collar behind bead and then apply a small amount of super glue to thread. Wrap thread several times so it sinks into the dubbing. Cut thread to finish. Super glue will secure thread.

Dry Spruce

Tied by Dean Reiner of Hatch Finders Fly Shop

HOOK:	Dai-Riki #320, size 10-14
THREAD:	Red Uni 6/0
TAIL:	Four or five strains of black moose
RIB:	Fine silver wire
BODY:	Red thread tightly wrapped and tapered to the thorax, then reverse- wrapped with fine silver wire
THORAX:	Two strands of peacock herl
HACKLE:	Badger dry-fly hackle
WINGS:	Badger hackle tips

Iris Caddis

Tied by Blue Ribbon Flies

HOOK:	Tiemco #2488 or 102Y, size 14-20
THREAD:	Rusty dun Uni 8/0
SHUCK:	Caddisfly amber or caddisfly gold-dyed Z-Lon
ABDOMEN:	Amber, tan, or olive Z-Lon Dubbing, (amber in photo)
WING:	Loop of white Z-Lon
HEAD:	Hare's ear dubbing

Jack Cabe

Tied by Yellowstone Fly Goods

HOOK:	Daiichi #1270 or TMC #200R, size 8-12
THREAD:	Black Uni 6/0
TAIL:	Red calf tail
WING:	Light tan calf tail
BODY:	Mottled brown mohair
HACKLE:	Brown and grizzly saddle hackle
OPTIONS:	Speckled legs

Kingfisher MFC Widow Maker Golden Stone

Tied by Montana Fly Company

HOOK:	3XL bronze MFC #7027, size 8
THREAD:	Dark brown Uni
BODY:	MFC brown/tan Furry Foam Bodies, size 6-8
LEGS:	Speckled tan MFC Centipede Legs
WING:	Caddis tan and dark brown MFC Widow's Web mixed and tied on each segment
INDICATOR:	Hot pink MFC Swisher's Gator Hair
HACKLE:	Grizzly dyed dark tan
THORAX:	Natural peacock herl

Mystery Meat Salmonfly

Tied by Dan Bailey

HOOK:	Dai-Riki #700, size 4-8
THREAD:	Wapsi 70-denier fluorescent fire orange
TAIL:	Medium black rubber legs
OVERBODY:	Brown 2mm foam
UNDERBODY:	Rust 2mm Foam
WING:	Dark elk with pearl Krystal Flash
HEAD:	Black elk hair
INDICATOR:	Orange 2mm foam
BODY HACKLE:	Medium dun

Olive Comparadun Baetis

Tied by Dan Bailey

HOOK:	Dai-Riki #310, size 16-22
THREAD:	Olive 8/0
TAIL:	Olive Microfibetts
WING:	Natural coastal deer hair
BODY:	Blue-wing olive dubbing
HEAD:	Blue-wing olive dubbing

Olive Foam-Back Caddis

Tied by Dan Bailey

HOOK:	Dai-Riki #300, size 12-16
THREAD:	Olive 8/0
WING:	Natural dark elk
BODY:	Olive fine dubbing
FOAM BACK/SHELL:	Olive 1mm foam
RIBBING:	Brown thread 3/0
HEAD:	Olive 1mm foam
INDICATOR:	Orange 1mm foam
THORAX:	Peacock Angel Hair

Olive Snowshoe Baetis

Tied by Yellowstone Fly Goods

HOOK:	Standard dry-fly, size 16-22
THREAD:	Olive dun Uni 8/0
TAIL:	Rusty brown Antron or Z-Lon
WING:	Dub snowshoe rabbit foot
BODY:	YFG Spectrum blue-wing olive dubbing
OPTIONS:	Pale morning dun or gray dubbing

Olive Stimulator

Tied by Dan Bailey

HOOK:	Dai-Riki #270, size 6-16
THREAD:	Fire orange 6/0
TAIL:	Dark elk hair
WING:	Dark elk hair
BODY:	Olive dry-fly dubbing
HACKLE:	Grizzly
RIBBING:	Fine gold wire
THORAX:	Orange Fly Rite dubbing
BODY HACKLE:	Brown

Oswald's Golden Rastaman

Tied by Montana Fly Company

HOOK:	3XL bronze MFC #7027, size 6
THREAD:	Tan Nymo
TAIL:	Natural whitetail deer flank
EGG SAC:	Black 2mm foam
RIB:	Tan Nymo thread
BODY:	Golden stone MFC Frog's Hair
UNDERWING:	Brown CDC
WING:	Tan CDC
HEAD AND COLLAR:	Gold cow elk flank
LEGS:	Speckled tan MFC Centipede Legs
INDICATOR:	Orange 1mm foam
TOP INDICATOR:	Yellow 1mm foam

Pale Morning Dun Biot Parachute

Tied by Dan Bailey

HOOK:	Dai-Riki #320, size 16-20
THREAD:	Light yellow 10/0
TAIL:	White Microfibetts
WING:	White Antron yarn
BODY:	Pale morning dun turkey biot
THORAX:	Pale morning dun dubbing
HACKLE:	Light dun

Perry's Bugmeister

Tied by Montana Fly Company

HOOK:	2XL light-wire bronze MFC #7022 size 8
THREAD:	Dark brown Uni
POST:	White MFC Widow's Web
TAIL:	Natural cow elk flank
BODY:	Natural peacock herl
UNDERWING:	Pearl Flashabou Accent
WING:	Natural cow elk flank
THORAX:	Natural peacock herl
HACKLE:	Grizzly

Royal Coachman Trude

Tied by Dan Bailey

HOOK:	Dai-Riki #305, size 8-16
THREAD:	Black 6/0
TAIL:	Golden pheasant tippet
WING:	White calf tail
BODY:	Peacock herl with a band of red floss in the middle
HACKLE:	Coachman brown

Royal Convertible

Tied by Dan Bailey

HOOK:	Dai-Riki #730, size 10-14
THREAD:	Fire orange 6/0
TAIL:	Moose body hair
WING:	White calf tail
BODY:	Dark olive dubbing with fire orange thread
HACKLE:	Brown
LEGS:	Black medium rubber

Royal Wulff

Tied by Dan Bailey

HOOK:	Dai-Riki #300, size 8-20
THREAD:	Black 6/0
TAIL:	Dark elk mane
WING:	White calf tail
BODY:	Peacock herl with a band of red floss in the middle
HACKLE:	Coachman brown

Yellow Parachute Madam X

Tied by Dan Bailey

HOOK:	Dai-Riki #730, size 10-14
THREAD:	Yellow 6/0
LEGS:	White silicone legs
TAIL:	Light elk hair
WING:	Light elk hair
BODY:	Yellow floss
THORAX:	Dark olive synthetic dubbing
POST:	White Hi-Vis Floater
HACKLE:	Grizzly

Silverman's Orange Crystal Stimi

Tied by Montana Fly Company

HOOK:	Bronze Stimi MFC #7002, size 12
THREAD:	Orange Uni
TAIL:	Bleached cow elk flank
RIB:	Copper wire
PALMER HACKLE:	Brown
BODY:	Orange Wings-n-Flash
UNDERWING:	Pearl Flashabou Accent
OVERWING:	Bleached cow elk flank
LEGS:	Orange Barbed Wire Silly Legs
THORAX HACKLE:	Brown
THORAX:	Orange Wings-n-Flash

Silverman's Para-Sally

Tied by Montana Fly Company

HOOK:	2XL bronze MFC #7026, size 14
THREAD:	Yellow Uni
POST:	White MFC Swisher's Gator Hair
EGG SAC:	Red Uni thread
BODY:	Pale morning dun MFC Frog's Hair
WING:	Pearl Flashabou Accent doubled over
THORAX:	Pale morning dun MFC Frog's Hair
HACKLE:	Ginger

Sparkle Dun

Tied by Blue Ribbon Flies

HOOK:	Tiemco #100 or 2488, size 12-24
THREAD:	Uni 8/0
SHUCK:	Mayfly brown or olive-dyed Z-Lon
ABDOMEN:	Nature's Finest or Super Fine dubbing to match natural (pale morning dun in photo). This pattern is tied to match any and all mayfly emergences from PMDs and green drakes to Baetis (tiny western olives) and mahogany duns.
WING:	Deer hair dyed dun or natural to match natural

Swisher's Original PMX

Tied by Montana Fly Company

HOOK:	2XL light-wire bronze MFC #7022, size 10
THREAD:	Black Uni
POST:	White MFC Widow's Web
TAIL:	Natural cow elk flank
ABDOMEN:	Golden stone MFC Swisher's Gator Hair
WING:	Natural cow elk flank
HACKLE:	Grizzly
LEGS:	White MFC Centipede Legs
THORAX:	Natural peacock herl

Tent-Wing Cinnamon Caddis

Tied By Dean Reiner of Hatch Finders Fly Shop

HOOK:	Dai-Riki #320, size 10-18
THREAD:	Black Uni 8/0
BODY:	Super Fine cinnamon caddisfly dubbing
HACKLE:	Light dun dry fly
WING:	Montana Fly Company wing material mottled brown #520 (use MFC Caddis cutter set #8-18)
ANTENNAE:	Striped grizzly hackle stems

Traveling Swede

Tied by Dean Reiner of Hatch Finders Fly Shop

HOOK:	Dai-Riki #320, size 10
THREAD:	Orange Uni 8/0
BODY:	Tie in this order—a thin strip of yellow foam, brown dry-fly hackle, thin strip of orange foam; wrap forward orange foam to three-quarters of hook shank, reverse-wrap brown hackle, cover hackle with yellow foam and tie off
WING:	Dark bull elk

Trina's Carnage Golden Stone

Tied by Montana Fly Company

HOOK:	2XL bronze light-wire MFC #7022, size 8
THREAD:	Tan Uni
TAIL:	Brown goose biot
ABDOMEN:	Tan 1mm foam
WING:	Mottled-web MFC Etha-Wing
OVERWING:	Smoke MFC Widow's Web
THORAX:	Golden yellow Antron Super Bright dubbing
HEAD:	Natural cow elk flank hair
LEGS:	Brown MFC Centipede Legs
INDICATOR:	Yellow foam

Trina's Etha-Wing Pale Morning Dun

Tied by Montana Fly Company

HOOK:	Standard dry-fly bronze MFC #7000, size 14
THREAD:	Light Cahill Uni 6/0
TAIL:	White Microfibbetts
ABDOMEN:	PMD MFC Frog's Hair
WING:	Dun MFC Etha-Wing
WING CASE:	Yellow Wings-n-Flash (small dubbed ball to divide wings)
LEGS:	Tan MFC Tentacles #2
HACKLE:	Cream
THORAX:	PMD MFC Frog's Hair

Trina's Noble Chernobyl Salmonfly

Tied by Montana Fly Company

HOOK:	3XL bronze MFC #7027, size 4
THREAD:	Black Nymo
UNDERBODY:	Orange foam
OVERBODY:	Black foam
WING:	Natural cow elk flank
INDICATOR:	Yellow foam
BACK LEGS:	Black MFC Centipede Legs
FRONT LEGS:	Black MFC Centipede Legs
POST:	White MFC Widow's Web
HACKLE:	Grizzly

Trina's Orange Stimi Chew-Toy

Tied by Montana Fly Company

HOOK:	Bronze Stimi MFC #7002, size 8
THREAD:	Orange Uni
TAIL:	Natural cow elk flank
RIB:	Copper wire
PALMER HACKLE:	Brown
ABDOMEN:	Orange Antron dubbing
UNDERWING:	MFC Mottled-Web MFC Etha-Wing
WING:	Natural cow elk flank
X LEGS:	Speckled Orange MFC Centipede Legs
THORAX:	Orange Wings-n-Flash
FRONT HACKLE:	Grizzly

Trina's Yellow Stimi Chew-Toy

Tied by Montana Fly Company

HOOK:	Bronze Stimi MFC #7002, size 8
THREAD:	Yellow Uni
TAIL:	Natural cow elk flank
RIB:	Copper wire
PALMER HACKLE:	Brown
ABDOMEN:	Yellow Antron dubbing
UNDERWING:	Mottled-Web MFC Etha-Wing
WING:	Natural cow elk flank
X LEGS:	Speckled yellow MFC Centipede Legs
THORAX:	Yellow Wings-n-Flash
FRONT HACKLE:	Grizzly

X Caddis

Tied by Blue Ribbon Flies

HOOK:	Tiemco #100, size 14-20
THREAD:	Rusty dun Uni 8/0
SHUCK:	Caddisfly gold or amber-dyed Z-Lon
BODY:	Tan, olive, black or amber Z-Lon dubbing blend to match natural (tan in photo)
WING:	Mottled deer hair
HEAD:	Trimmed butts of the wing of the fly

Yellow Goofus Bug

Tied by Dan Bailey

HOOK:	Dai-Riki #300, size 8-18
THREAD:	Yellow 6/0
TAIL:	Deer body hair
WING/SHELLBACK:	Deer body hair
BODY:	Yellow floss
HACKLE:	Grizzly and brown

Bead-Head Hare's Ear

Tied by Dan Bailey

HOOK:	Dai-Riki #730, size 10-18
THREAD:	Gray 6/0
TAIL:	Guard hairs from hare's mask
WING CASE:	Oak-mottled turkey wing
BODY:	Hare's ear dubbing
RIBBING:	Small oval gold tinsel
HEAD:	Gold bead
THORAX:	Hare's ear dubbing
WEIGHT:	Lead wire

Bead-Head Pheasant Tail Nymph

Tied by Dan Bailey

HOOK:	Dai-Riki #135, size 12-18
THREAD:	Olive 8/0
TAIL:	Pheasant tail
WING CASE:	Pheasant tail
BODY:	Pheasant tail
HEAD:	Gold bead
THORAX:	Peacock herl
LEGS:	Natural pheasant tail fibers
RIB:	Small copper wire

Bead-Head Prince Nymph

Tied by Dan Bailey

HOOK:	Dai-Riki #730, size 10-16
THREAD:	Black 8/0
TAIL:	Brown goose biots
RIBBING:	Small oval gold tinsel
WEIGHT:	Lead wire
BODY:	Peacock eye feathers
WING:	White goose biots
HACKLE:	Brown partridge
HEAD:	Gold bead

Bitch Creek Nymph

Tied by Dan Bailey

HOOK:	Dai-Riki #710, size 2-10
THREAD:	Black 6/0
TAIL/ANTENNAE:	White medium rubber legs
BODY:	Black chenille and light orange chenille
HACKLE:	Brown saddle
THORAX:	Black chenille
WEIGHT:	Lead wire

Black and Red Rolling Stone

Tied by Yellowstone Fly Goods

HOOK:	Daiichi #1150, size 8-12
THREAD:	Black Uni 6/0
TAIL:	Black Crazy Legs
BODY:	Black and red wire
WING CASE:	Black Body Stretch
THORAX:	Peacock Highlight Dubbing
LEGS:	Black Crazy Legs
OPTIONS:	Copper and gold wire

Copper John Nymph

Tied by Dan Bailey

HOOK:	Dai-Riki #730, size 12-18
THREAD:	Black 8/0
TAIL:	Brown goose biots
BODY:	Copper wire
WING CASE:	Pearl tinsel and epoxy on top
WEIGHT:	Lead wire
LEGS:	Pheasant tail
BEAD:	Gold
THORAX:	Peacock herl

Delektable Black Orange-Legs Bug

Tied by Riverborn Fly Company

HOOK:	Daiichi #1730 stonefly-nymph, size 6-10
THREAD:	Black waxed Danville 3/0
ANTENNAE:	Orange Sili Legs with black barring
HEAD:	Gold bead (wrap a little dubbing before adding bead)
TAIL:	Black marabou
WEIGHT:	.030-inch-diameter tin wire along one side of the hook shank and then counter-wrapped from back to front
BODY:	Copper, gold and black Riverborn New Age chenille
LEGS:	Orange Sili Legs with black barring
HACKLE:	Black hen

Delektable CDC Baby

Tied by Riverborn Fly Company

HOOK:	Daiichi #1120 wide-gape scud, size 6-16
HEAD:	Gold bead to match size of hook
THREAD:	Dark brown waxed Danville 6/0
TAG:	Chartreuse-colored 100 percent Acrylic yarn
RIBBING:	Small amber Ultra Wire for hooks size 12-14, medium for hooks 6-10
BODY:	Four strands of peacock herl for hooks size 12-16, six strands for hooks 6-10
HACKLE:	Medium brown CDC—longer, fuller hackle for size 12-16 hooks; smaller, sparser hackle for hooks 18-20
LEGS:	Nymph-size solid brown Sili Legs
WING:	Rust-colored 2-Ply Yarn
COLLAR:	Peacock Ice Dub behind bead. Apply a small amount of super glue to thread and then wrap several times to sink into dubbing. Cut thread to finish. Super glue will secure thread.

Delektable Mega Prince Olive Flashback

Tied by Riverborn Fly Company

HOOK:	Daiichi #1730 stonefly-nymph hook, size 6-10
BEAD:	Copper bead
WEIGHT:	.025-inch diameter tin tied in strips along both sides of the hook and then counter-wrapped from back to front
THREAD:	Black waxed Danville 6/0
TAIL:	Brown grizzly marabou
TAG:	Regular-size pumpkin, green and orange Sili Legs
RIBBING:	Copper wire
BODY:	Peacock herl over a strip of .030-inch-diameter tin wire along each side of the hook shank
WING CASE:	Twenty strands of pearl Krystal Flash coated with clear epoxy
HACKLE:	Brown sparkled hen back
HORNS:	Olive goose biot
COLLAR:	Peacock Ice Dubbing. Dub collar behind bead and then apply a small amount of super glue to thread. Wrap thread several times so thread sinks into dubbing and cut thread to finish. Super glue will secure thread.

Double-Bead Black Stonefly

Tied by Riverborn Fly Company

HOOK:	Daiichi #1730 stonefly-nymph hook, size 4-10
THREAD:	Black waxed Danville 6/0
WEIGHT:	.025-inch-diameter tin (if extra weight is needed)
RIBBING:	Black V-Rib
BODY:	Black mohair
THORAX:	Gold bead, then dubbing, then another gold bead (gaps between the beads should be the width of one bead)
LEGS:	Black round rubber
FEELER:	V-split black biot

Glass-Bead Quill Nymph

Tied by Yellowstone Fly Goods

HOOK:	Heavy nymph, size 18-20
THREAD:	Black Uni 8/0
BEAD:	Peacock glass
TAIL:	Pheasant tail
RIBBING:	Fine silver wire
BODY:	Black Uni 8/0 thread
WING CASE:	Pearlescent tinsel
THORAX:	Peacock herl
OPTIONS:	No bead

Glass-House Caddis

Tied by Dan Bailey

HOOK:	Dai-Riki #060, size 10-14
THREAD:	Black 6/0
BODY:	Dark olive dubbing
RIB:	Fine copper wire
HEAD:	Green glass bead, black bead
HACKLE:	Brown India hen

Hare's Ear Double-Bead Stone

Tied by Montana Fly Company

HOOK:	3XL bent-shank bronze MFC #7073, size 8
BEADS:	Gold
THREAD:	Black Uni
TAIL:	Cream goose biot
RIB:	Clear mono
ABDOMEN:	Natural hare's ear dubbing
WING CASE:	Natural wild turkey tail
THORAX:	Natural hare's ear dubbing
LEGS:	Cream goose biot

Kyle's Beer-Head Baetis

Tied by Montana Fly Company

HOOK:	Bronze scud hook MFC #7045, size 16
GLASS BEAD:	Root Beer, size 11/0
THREAD:	Tan Uni 8/0
TAIL:	Brown Hungarian partridge
RIB:	Size 0 copper wire
BACK:	Flat pearl Mylar tinsel
BODY:	Callibaetis MFC Frog's Hair
WING CASE:	Flat pearl Mylar tinsel
LEGS:	Brown Hungarian partridge

Kyle's Bead-Head Yellow Sally

Tied by Montana Fly Company

BEAD:	Gold
HOOK:	2XL bronze MFC #7026, size 12
THREAD:	Tan Uni
TAIL:	Brown goose biot
RIB:	Copper wire
BACK:	Burnt orange MFC Gator Hair
ABDOMEN:	Light Cahill MFC Frog's Hair dubbing
WING CASE:	Black trash bag
ANTENNAE:	Brown goose biot
THORAX:	Yellow Wings-n-Flash
LEGS:	Gray Hungarian partridge divided

Nature Stone Nymph

Tied by Blue Ribbon Flies

HOOK:	Gamakatsu #C12U or Mustad #37160, size 6-8
THREAD:	Black Uni 6/0
TAILS:	Dyed brown stripped goose biots
ABDOMEN:	Black Z-Lon dubbing blend
RIB:	Fine black V Rib
UNDERBELLY:	Bright orange wool yarn
WING CASES, PRONOTUM (DORSAL PLATE) AND HEAD:	Dyed black latex trimmed to shape
THORAX:	Black Z-Lon dubbing
LEGS:	Pheasant back feathers from between wings, well mottled
ANTENNAE:	Dyed brown stripped goose biots

Oswald's Bead-Head Rock Roller

Tied by Montana Fly Company

HOOK:	3LX bent-shank bronze MFC #7073, size 10
BEAD:	Black
THREAD:	Black Uni
WEIGHT:	Lead wire
BODY:	Gold and silver MFC High Voltage, white, tan, brown and black MFC Centipede Legs well mixed and spun around the hook like deer hair
HEAD:	Black MFC Wabbit dubbing in dubbing loop

Rainbow Serendipity

Tied by Yellowstone Fly Goods

HOOK:	Scud Daichi #1120, Tiemco #2457 or Dai Riki #135 size 12-18
THREAD:	Tan Uni 8/0
BODY:	Twisted pearl Krystal Flash
RIBBING:	Fine gold wire
WING:	Light deer hair
HEAD:	Clipped light deer hair

$3 Bridge Serendipity

Tied by Blue Ribbon Flies

HOOK:	Tiemco #3761 or 2488, size 14-18
THREAD:	Danville #47 6/0
BODY:	Working thread
RIB:	Fine gold wire
WING CASE:	Trimmed deer hair butts
OPTION:	Gold bead head

Trina's Copperback Stone

Tied by Montana Fly Company

HOOK:	3XL bent-shank bronze MFC #7073, size 8
BEAD:	Gold
THREAD:	Rusty brown Uni
WEIGHT:	Lead wire
TAIL:	Brown goose biot
UNDERBODY:	Golden brown MFC Frog's Hair dubbing
BODY:	Black and copper wire wrapped together
WING CASE:	mottled-web MFC wing material coated with clear epoxy
THORAX:	Rust and golden amber MFC Wabbit dubbing mixed with golden stone Z-Lon
LEGS:	Brown goose biot

Black Cone-Head Yuk Bug

Tied by Yellowstone Fly Goods

HOOK:	3X streamer, size 2-8
CONE:	Gunmetal
THREAD:	Black Flymaster+
TAIL:	Gray squirrel tail
FLASH:	Pearl Krystal Flash
BODY:	Black chenille
RIBBING:	Medium silver wire
LEGS:	Black and smoke Speckled Legs
HACKLE:	Grizzly saddle

Chocolate Mint Bead-Head Bugger

Tied by Riverborn Fly Company

HOOK:	Daiichi #1720 2XL 2X strong, size 4-10
THREAD:	Black waxed Danville 3/0
HEAD:	Gold bead
TAIL:	Brown and olive marabou fluff the length of the hook shank with two pieces of pearl Flashabou on each side
RIBBING:	Small-size brown Ultra Wire counter-wrapped
BODY:	Riverborn New Age chocolate mint chenille wound very tightly
COLLAR:	Green peacock dubbing just behind the bead
HACKLE:	Dark brown saddle

Coffey's Peacock Sparkle Minnow

Tied by Montana Fly Company

HOOK:	2XL bronze MFC #7026, size 4
THREAD:	.20-inch clear mono
BEAD:	Gold
WEIGHT:	.8mm lead wire
TAIL:	Olive Brown marabou blood quill
FLASH IN TAIL:	Pearl dyed black, root beer and ultraviolet gray Flashabou Accent
UNDERBODY:	Peacock Angel Hair
BODY:	Peacock Angel Hair in a dubbing loop and wrapped

Coffey's CH Sculpin Sparkle Minnow

Tied by Montana Fly Company

HOOK:	4XL bronze MFC #7008, size 6
CONE:	Black
THREAD:	Tan Nymo
WEIGHT:	Lead wire
FLASH:	Copper Flashabou Accent
BOTTOM TAIL:	White marabou
MIDDLE TAIL:	Tan marabou
TOP TAIL:	Olive brown marabou
BOTTOM BODY:	Pearl Wings-n-Flash in dubbing loop pulled forward
MIDDLE BODY:	Gold Wings-n-Flash in a dubbing loop and wrapped
TOP BODY:	Black permanent marker

Cone-Head Rubber Bugger Takillya

Tied by Montana Fly Company

HOOK:	4XL bronze MFC #7008, size 4
THREAD:	Brown Nymo
CONE:	Gold
WEIGHT:	Lead wire
BOTTOM TAIL:	Yellow marabou
TOP TAIL:	Dark brown marabou
FLASH:	Six strands copper MFC High Voltage
BODY:	Root beer Estaz
HACKLE:	Yellow/Brown MFC Rubber Hackle

Delektable Black Double Screamer

Tied by Riverborn Fly Company

BACK OR TRAILER HOOK:	Daiichi #2220 4XL 1X heavy, size 6
THREAD:	Black waxed Danville 3/0 or heavier
TAIL:	One large plume of black marabou with four black saddle hackles paired up and split over the marabou—hackles should flare out. Add two strips of silver holographic tinsel on each side of the black saddle hackles.
BODY:	Lite Brite Northern Lights
HEAD TOPPING:	One large plume of black marabou
HEAD:	Light Brite Baitfish dubbing. Dub head and then apply a small amout of super glue to thread. Wrap several times so thread sinks into the dubbing. Cut thread to finish. Super glue will secure thread.

Delektable Black Double Screamer (continued)

Tied by Riverborn Fly Company

* * *

FRONT HOOK:	Daiichi #2220 4XL 1X heavy, size 6—connect assembled trailer hook (above) with 15-pound-test fluorocarbon monofilament allowing a half-inch gap between hooks.
WEIGHT:	.025-inch-diameter tin wire wound as an underbody
CONE HEAD:	Large gold cone
TAIL:	One large plume of black marabou with four black saddle hackles paired up and split over the marabou—hackles should flare out. Add two strips of silver holographic tinsel on each side of the black saddle hackles.
BODY:	Lite Brite Northern Lights
HEAD TOPPING:	One large plume of black marabou tied in on top of hook shank
HACKLE COLLAR:	Two black hackles wound behind cone
COLLAR:	Lite Brite Baitfish dubbing. Dub head and then apply a small amount of super glue to thread. Wrap several times so thread sinks into the dubbing. Cut thread to finish. Super glue will secure thread.

Delektable Spawning Screamer

Tied by Riverborn Fly Company

HOOK:	Daiichi #2220 4XL 1X heavy, size 6
THREAD:	Black waxed Danville 3/0 or heavier
HEAD:	Large gold cone
WEIGHT:	.025-inch-diameter tin wire wound as an underbody
TAIL:	One plume of olive-dyed grizzly over one plume of white marabou with four grizzly saddle hackles dyed gray. Pair up the grizzly hackles and split over the marabou—the hackles should flare out.
BODY AND HEAD TOPPING:	Lite Brite Baitfish dubbing
WING:	One large yellow marabou plume tied on top of hook shank, followed by two red-dyed grizzly plumes tied one on each side of the shank, followed by two gray-dyed grizzly hackles—one on each side. The grizzly hackle should flare out from the marabou.
FLASH WING:	Six strands of gold Flashabou tied in after wing
HACKLE COLLAR:	Two gray-dyed grizzly saddle hackles wound behind cone
COLLAR:	Lite Brite Baitfish dubbing. Dub head and then apply a small amount of super glue to thread. Wrap thread several times so thread sinks into dubbing. Cut thread to finish. Super glue will secure thread.

Kyle's Olive Super Yummy

Tied by Montana Fly Company

HOOK:	6XL bronze MFC #7030, size 4
THREAD:	Olive Nymo
WEIGHT:	Lead wire
LEAD EYES:	Gold brass eyes recessed
EYES:	Gold Lure Eyes
TAIL:	Olive brown marabou
FLASH:	Pearl dyed black Flashabou Accent
RIB:	Gold wire
BODY:	Olive Estaz
LEGS:	Black MFC Centipede Legs
WING:	Olive rabbit hide

Muddler Minnow

Tied by Dan Bailey

HOOK:	Dai-Riki #710, size 2-12
THREAD:	White 3/0
TAIL:	Oak-mottled turkey
BODY:	Flat gold tinsel
WING:	Brown calf tail, white calf tail, oak-mottled turkey wing
WEIGHT:	Lead wire
COLLAR:	Natural deer hair
HEAD:	Spun and trimmed natural deer hair

Powell's Natural Brown Bunny Sculpin

Tied by Montana Fly Company

HOOK:	4XL bronze MFC #7008, size 4
THREAD:	Tan Nymo
WEIGHT:	Lead wire
LEAD EYES:	Black brass eyes recessed
EYES:	Gold Lure Eyes
TAIL:	Black marabou
RIB:	Gold wire
UNDERBODY:	Cream Furry Foam
FLASH:	Pearl Flashabou Accent
WING:	Natural cottontail hair, back hair then belly, back then belly, ending with back all flared to 180 degrees
HEAD:	Natural brown rabbit dubbing

Rickard's Seal Bugger No. 2

Tied by Montana Fly Company

HOOK:	4XL bronze MFC #7008, size 8
THREAD:	Black Uni
WEIGHT:	Lead wire
TAIL:	Rickard's burgundy marabou
FLASH:	Two strands pearl MFC High Voltage
RIB:	Copper wire
BODY:	Black Rickard's Seal Sub dubbing mixed 75 percent with 25 percent Red Rickard's Seal Sub dubbing
HACKLE:	Grizzly dyed purple

Rickard's Seal Bugger No. 4

Tied by Montana Fly Company

HOOK:	4XL bronze MFC #7008, size 8
THREAD:	Black Uni
WEIGHT:	Lead wire
TAIL:	Rickard's burnt orange marabou
FLASH:	Two strands pearl MFC High Voltage
RIB:	Copper wire
BODY:	Dark olive Rickard's Seal Sub dubbing
HACKLE:	Grizzly dyed burnt orange

Ritt's Rust Fighting Crawfish

Tied by Montana Fly Company

HOOK:	3XL bronze bent-shank MFC # 7073, size 4
THREAD:	Rusty Brown Uni 6/0
EYES:	Lead eyes
WEIGHT:	8mm lead wire
CLAWS:	Orange 5mm foam
EYES:	Black MFC Centipede Legs
BODY:	Amber Angora goat mixed with rust MFC Wabbit dubbing
RIB:	Red wire
BACK:	Mottled orange MFC Skinny Skin
HACKLE:	Grizzly dyed burnt orange
LEGS:	Speckled orange MFC Centipede Legs
ANTENNA:	Orange mixed with ultraviolet gray Flashabou Accent

Spuddler

Tied by Dan Bailey

HOOK:	Dai-Riki #1155, size 2-8
THREAD:	Red 3/0
TAIL:	Brown calf tail
WEIGHT:	Lead wire
BODY:	Light yellow yarn
WING:	Brown calf tail, grizzly hackle dyed brown, natural-red fox squirrel tail
THROAT:	Red thread
COLLAR:	Natural deer hair
HEAD:	Spun and trimmed natural deer hair and natural brown antelope hair

Adams Midge Cluster

Tied by Yellowstone Fly Goods

HOOK:	Wide-gape dry-fly, size 16-20
THREAD:	Black Uni 8/0
WING:	Black Antron
BODY:	Brown and grizzly saddle hackle

Z-Lon Midge

Tied by Blue Ribbon Flies

HOOK:	Tiemco #2488 or 100, size 18-26
THREAD:	Olive dun Uni 8/0
SHUCK:	Midge gray or dark dun-dyed Z-Lon
BODY:	Working thread wraps over Z-Lon shuck
WING:	Midge gray or dark dun-dyed straight Z-Lon

Black Foam Beetle

Tied by Yellowstone Fly Goods

HOOK:	Standard dry-fly, size 12-18
THREAD:	Black Uni 8/0
INDICATOR:	Orange Fly Foam
WING CASE:	Black Fly Foam
BODY:	Peacock herl
LEGS:	Moose mane

Cinnamon Para Ant

Tied by Montana Fly Company

HOOK:	Standard dry-fly bronze MFC #7000, size 14
THREAD:	Rusty Brown Uni 6/0
ABDOMEN:	Camel MFC Frog's Hair
POST:	Golden stone MFC Widow's Web
THORAX:	Camel MFC Frog's Hair
HACKLE:	Grizzly

Dave's Hopper

Tied by Dan Bailey

HOOK:	Dai-Riki #730, size 4-14
THREAD:	Gray 6/0
TAIL:	Red deer hair
WING:	Mottled turkey wing
BODY:	Yellow yarn
HEAD:	Natural deer hair
COLLAR:	Tips of deer hair
BODY HACKLE:	Brown saddle
LEGS:	Grizzly dyed yellow hackle

Lady Bug

Tied By Dean Reiner of Hatch Finders Fly Shop

HOOK:	Dai-Riki #070, size 16
THREAD:	Black Uni 8/0
BODY:	Two strands of peacock herl
BACK:	Orange foam
SPOTS:	Black Sharpie pen

Pink Pookie

Tied by Dean Reiner of Hatch Finders Fly Shop

HOOK:	Dai-Riki #280, size 6-10
THREAD:	Red Uni 6/0
BODY:	Pink foam segmented with red thread (use Chernobyl-style foam body cutter set #2-12)
WING:	Light elk under tan foam—tie foam forward over the hook eye, apply a small drop of Zap-A-Gap, then fold back over body of the fly and tie off
LEGS:	Medium yellow Centipede Legs
INDICATOR:	Bright orange foam

Spider

Tied By Dean Reiner of Hatch Finders Fly Shop

HOOK:	Dai-Riki #280, size 14
THREAD:	Rusty brown 8/0
BODY:	Tie in tan foam midway on hook past the bend of the hook and wrap solid with thread; fold foam forward and tie down to the eye to form the abdomen, then fold back to form the head and tie off at the end of the abdomen.
LEGS:	Striped grizzly hackle stems
INDICATOR:	White Widow's Web
	(Use a light brown Sharpie to mark the abdomen)

Tan Hybrid Hopper

Tied by Yellowstone Fly Goods

HOOK:	3X streamer, size 8-12
THREAD:	Yellow Uni 6/0
LEGS:	Yellow braided mono
BODY:	Sandwiched tan and yellow foam
UNDERWING:	Gold swiss straw
WING:	Natural elk hair
OPTIONS:	Yellow belly

Taylor's Black Fat Albert

Tied by Montana Fly Company

HOOK:	3XL bronze MFC #7027, size 10
THREAD:	Black Uni
OVERBODY:	Black foam
UNDERBODY:	Black foam
REAR LEGS:	Black MFC Centipede Legs
UNDERWING:	Pearl MFC High Voltage
WING:	White MFC Widow's Web
INDICATOR:	Red foam
FRONT LEGS:	Black MFC Centipede Legs

Taylor's Yellow Fat Albert

Tied by Montana Fly Company

HOOK:	3XL bronze MFC #7027, size 8
THREAD:	Brown Nymo
OVERBODY:	Brown foam
UNDERBODY:	Yellow foam
REAR LEGS:	Speckled tan MFC Centipede Legs
UNDERWING:	Pearl MFC High Voltage
WING:	White MFC Widow's Web
INDICATOR:	Yellow foam
FRONT LEGS:	Speckled tan MFC Centipede Legs

Trina's Carnage Hopper

Tied by Montana Fly Company

HOOK:	2XL bronze light-wire MFC #7022, size 8
THREAD:	Tan Uni
ABDOMEN:	Tan 1mm foam
WING:	Montana Fly Company mottled-web wing material
BACK LEGS:	Clear Tan MFC Centipede Legs colored with marker
INDICATOR:	White MFC Widow's Web
HEAD:	Tan foam
LEGS:	Clear tan MFC Centipede Legs
THORAX:	Golden tan Antron dubbing
EYES:	Black Mono-Eyes

Turck's Tarantula

Tied by Dan Bailey

HOOK:	Dai-Riki #710, size 6-12
THREAD:	Gray 3/0
TAIL:	Amherst pheasant tippets
WING:	White calf body hair
BODY:	Natural hare's ear dubbing
HEAD:	Natural deer hair
LEGS:	Medium white rubber
LEGS:	Speckled tan MFC Centipede Legs

Ray Charles

Tied by Yellowstone Fly Goods

HOOK:	Heavy nymph, size 14-20
THREAD:	Fire orange Uni 8/0
WING CASE:	Pearlescent tinsel
BODY:	Gray ostrich herl
OPTIONS:	Tan or pink ostrich

Tan Poxyback Sowbug

Tied by Yellowstone Fly Goods

HOOK:	Heavy scud, size 16-20
THREAD:	Fire orange Uni 8/0
WING CASE:	Eighth-inch Body Stretch for scud back and holographic tinsel
BODY:	Tan Scud Dub
OPTIONS:	Gray or pink dubbing

Tan Soft-Hackle Ray Charles

Tied by Yellowstone Fly Goods, size 16-20

HOOK:	Heavy nymph
THREAD:	Fire orange Uni 8/0
RIBBING:	Fine silver wire
WING CASE:	Pearlescent tinsel
BODY:	Tan ostrich herl
HACKLE:	Gray hen neck
OPTIONS:	Gray or pink ostrich

Tan Soft-Hackle Sowbug

Tied by Yellowstone Fly Goods

HOOK:	Heavy nymph, size 14-20
THREAD:	Fire orange Uni 8/0
BODY:	Tan sowbug dubbing
HACKLE:	Gray neck hackle
OPTIONS:	Pink dubbing

Trina's Blue-Wing Olive Angel Case Emerger

Tied by Montana Fly Company

HOOK:	Bronze scud MFC #7045, size 16
BEAD:	Gold
THREAD:	Olive Uni
TAIL:	Natural ringneck pheasant tail
RIB:	Copper wire and one strand pearl Flashabou Accent
ABDOMEN:	Natural ringneck pheasant tail
WING:	Gun metal Wings-n-Flash rolled into a ball on a dubbing loop
THORAX:	Peacock Wings-n-Flash
LEGS:	Natural ringneck pheasant tail

Trina's Blue-Wing Olive Bubbleback Emerger

Tied by Montana Fly Company

HOOK:	Bronze scud MFC #7045, size 16
BEAD:	Gold
THREAD:	Olive Uni
TAIL:	Natural ringneck pheasant tail
RIB:	Copper wire and one strand black Flashabou Accent
ABDOMEN:	Natural ringneck pheasant tail
WING CASE:	Black Flashabou Accent
THORAX:	Peacock Wings-n-Flash
LEGS:	Black Flashabou Accent

Trina's Bubbleback Emerger

Tied by Montana Fly Company

HOOK:	Bronze scud MFC #7045, size 12
BEAD:	Gold
THREAD:	Rusty brown Uni
TAIL:	Natural ringneck pheasant tail
RIB:	Copper wire and one strand pearl Flashabou Accent
ABDOMEN:	Natural ringneck pheasant tail
WING CASE:	Natural ringneck pheasant tail and yellow Flashabou Accent
THORAX:	Natural peacock herl
LEGS:	Pearl Flashabou Accent

Trina's CDC Blue-Wing Olive Budding Emerger

Tied by Montana Fly Company

HOOK:	Light-wire bronze scud MFC #7048, size 18
THREAD:	Olive dun Uni
TAIL:	Brown MFC Z-Yarn
POST:	White 4mm MFC foam tube
ABDOMEN:	brown Super Floss and olive Tentacles wrapped together
THORAX:	Olive MFC Frog's Hair dubbing
HACKLE:	Dark dun MFC Henry's Fork Hackle

Trina's CDC Pale Morning Dun Budding Emerger

Tied by Montana Fly Company

HOOK:	Light-wire bronze scud MFC #7048, size 14
THREAD:	Light Cahill Uni
TAIL:	Rusty brown MFC Z-Yarn
ABDOMEN:	Cocoa brown MFC Spider Legs
POST:	White 4mm MFC foam tube
THORAX:	Pale morning dun MFC Frog's Hair dubbing
HACKLE:	Light dun MFC Henry's Fork Hackle

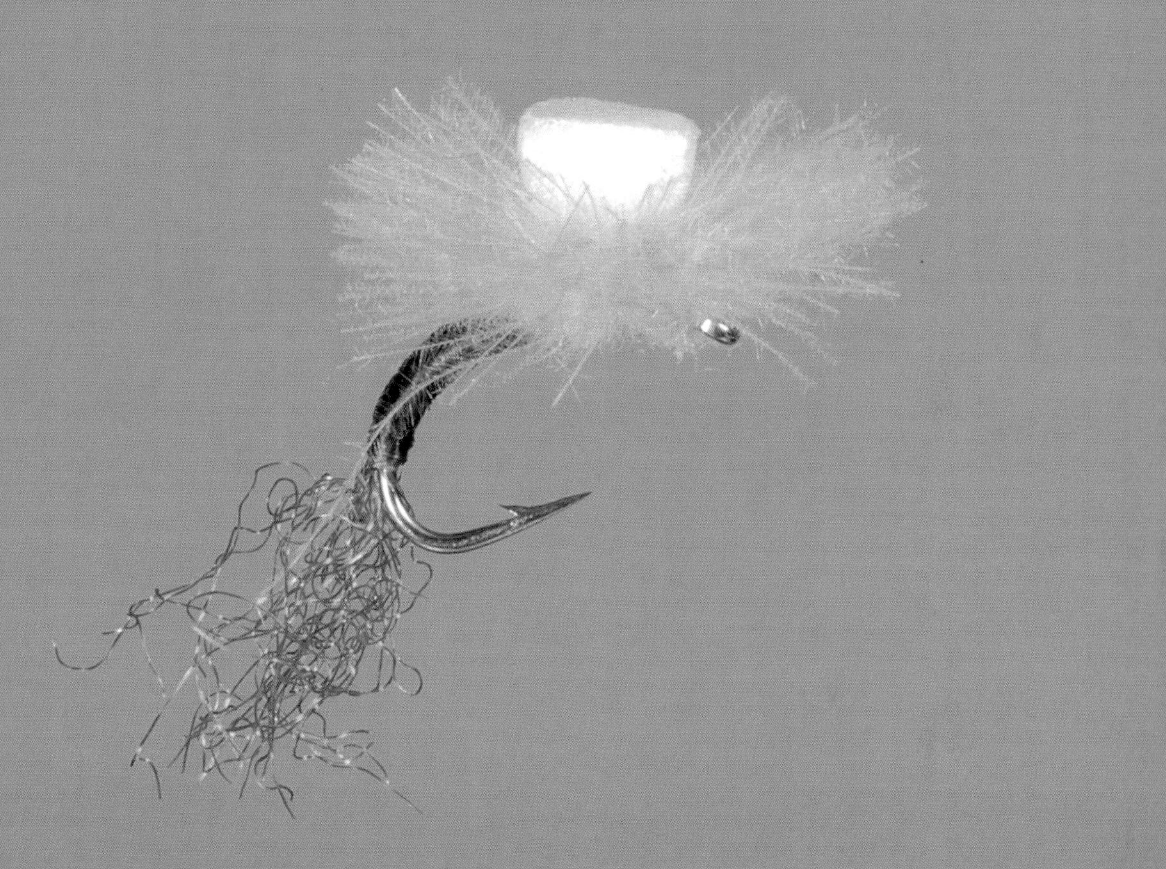

Trina's Pale Morning Dun Angel Case Emerger

Tied by Montana Fly Company

HOOK:	Bronze scud MFC #7045, size 16
BEAD:	Gold
THREAD:	Rusty brown Uni
TAIL:	Natural ringneck pheasant tail
RIB:	Copper wire and one strand pearl Flashabou Accent
ABDOMEN:	Natural ringneck pheasant tail
WING:	Yellow Wings-n-Flash rolled into a ball on a dubbing loop
THORAX:	Pale Morning Dun Wings-n-Flash
LEGS:	Natural ringneck pheasant tail

Trina's Pale Morning Dun Bubbleback Emerger

Tied by Montana Fly Company

HOOK:	Bronze scud MFC #7045, size 16
BEAD:	Gold
THREAD:	Light Cahill Uni
TAIL:	Natural ringneck pheasant
RIB:	Copper wire and one strand yellow Flashabou Accent
ABDOMEN:	Natural ringneck pheasant tail
WING CASE:	Natural ringneck pheasant tail and pearl Flashabou Accent
THORAX:	Yellow Wings-n-Flash
LEGS:	Yellow Flashabou Accent

Weamer's Western Green Drake Truform Emerger

Tied by Montana Fly Company

HOOK:	Trueform #1230-Bronze, size 10
THREAD:	Olive dun Uni 6/0
POST:	Olive brown MFC Z-Yarn
TAIL:	Dark brown MFC Z-Yarn
RIB:	Yellow Nymo thread
ABDOMEN:	Brown MFC Wabbit dubbing
ABDOMEN:	Light olive MFC Wabbit dubbing
WING:	Mixed black and medium dun CDC
THORAX:	Brown MFC Wabbit dubbing
THORAX:	Light Olive MFC Wabbit dubbing
HACKLE:	Grizzly dyed olive

Otter's Apricot Opaque Soft Milk Egg

Tied by Montana Fly Company

HOOK:	Bronze scud hook MFC #7045, size 12
THREAD:	Orange Uni
TAIL:	White Antron dubbing
BODY:	MFC Otter's Apricot opaque 6mm Soft Egg
VEIL:	White Antron dubbing

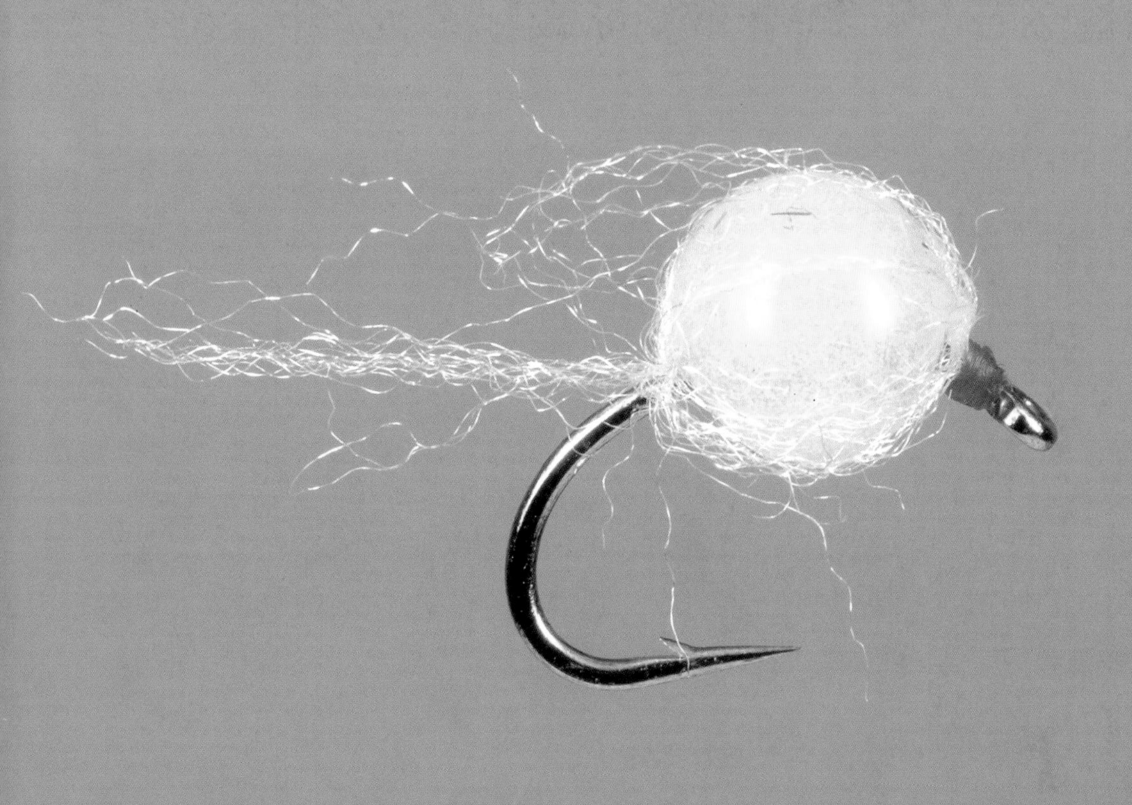

Dan Bailey
209 West Park Street
Livingston, Montana 59047
Telephone: 800-356-4052
Web site: www.dan-bailey.com

Blue Ribbon Flies
305 North Canyon Street
West Yellowstone, Montana 59758
Telephone: 406-646-7642
Web site: www.blueribbonflies.com

Hatch Finders Fly Shop
113 West Park Street, Suite 3
Livingston, Montana 59047
Telephone: 406-222-0989
Web site: www.hatchfinders.com

Montana Fly Company
530 First Avenue West
Columbia Falls, Montana 59912
Telephone: 406-892-9112
Web site: www.montanafly.com

Riverborn Fly Company
4464 West Chinden Boulevard, Suite C
Boise, Idaho 83717
Telephone: 800-354-5534
Web site: www.riverbornflies.com

Yellowstone Fly Goods
5350 Holiday Avenue
Billings, Montana 59101
Telephone: 800-262-3353
Web site: www.yellowstoneflygoods.com